Krishna's Anarchy

Alex Wylie
Krishna's Anarchy

POETRY

THE **BLACK SPRING**
PRESS GROUP

First published in 2023
by The Black Spring Press Group
Eyewear Publishing imprint
Maida Vale, London W9,
United Kingdom

Typeset with graphic design by Edwin Smet
Cover image by Shutterstock

ISBN 978-1-915406-30-9

BLACKSPRINGPRESSGROUP.COM

In memory of Ciaran Carson

Ché la diritta via era smarrita.

Alex Wylie is a senior lecturer at York St John University. He is also the author of *Secular Games* and *Geoffrey Hill's Later Work: Radiance of Apprehension*.

Table of Contents

While the residents of svarga looked on, Krishna, the enjoyer of sacrifice, took pleasure engaging in childish play. He carried a flute in the garments around his stomach, and a horn and staff in his belt. In his left hand was a tender morsel of food, and in his fingers were pieces of fruit. Standing in the middle of his circle of intimate friends, he made them laugh with his games.

Śrīmad-Bhagāvatam, Book 10, Chapter 13, Verse 11

Oh Krishna, mighty-armed Krishna... your father has been bound and taken away by Salva, like an animal by a butcher.

Śrīmad-Bhagāvatam, Book 10, Chapter 77, Verse 22

1

Sweets for breakfast, all the crap of the day
complete in one convenient sitting
like a read-through of some 'creative writing'
exercise, or speeded-up *Dies Irae*
at one hundred and fifty beats per minute.
One day, my beaten heart gives up on it,

packs in: the veins and arteries hardening
against me, outraged by saturated fats
as blood-purifying Caliphates
by booze, fast foods – the Government gives **WARNING**.
Something in the blood – white corpuscles
more terrorist sleeper than blood cells.

The air collapses also: late autumn;
unsentimental windshowers wring and pluck
the trees half-bare (Dutch elm disease, ash dieback),
the blasted habitats of Brock Bottom
shrinking back like gums; tooth-cogs; skeletons
revealed, assumed, bodily, into the heavens,

the fossils of the north: dead mothers; the kid
who should have been at school, or safe at home.
The poet's less intelligent than their poem:
mathematics to a teenage Euclid
sketching the circle. It's a guessing-
game in which foreknowing is foreclosing,

though an atmosphere gathers, like November fog
on frost-furrowed farmland repossessed by Lloyd's
of London. I stumbled through those clouds

as through hiss-buzzing swarms of analogue
static, cosmic background radiation
flooding the heads of a white-noisy nation,

cycled through, without a careful thought,
wobbling with imagination's unbalance.
Tractors were always Massey-Fergusons —
great red mammoths, bumbling, lost, throughout
the blunt country between the lakes and towns.
I trod in cowpats, went the wrong way. Once

you've made that first footprint, you can't go back
(I take as my example, here, Ted Hughes,
subject of that liberal *J'Accuse!*
of displaced accusation; shaman or quack;
hunter, butcher, murderer, hawk-fancier;
dark horse of the London intelligentsia;

his Sylvia not his Sylvia
but theirs, rising from the ash to eat
the heart out of the English laureate;
star-droplet of essential moonsilver
poised to drip from the furred camellia leaf
delicate, subjective, the pearl of grief).

The footprint in the mud is filled with rain.
The footprint on the moon sealed into dust
is perfect always. Galileo 'confessed'.
The Holy Spirit, the Father, and the Son
moved him, in their sacred depositions,
inspired his hand through those retrograde motions

regular as clockwork... But I digress.
Again. *Teste David cum Sibylla.*
Tom the farmer melts into his Celia

underground. They had a sheepdog called Jess.
Yes, it rhymes... But it happens to be true.
Caravans hunched beneath the wishing-tree

in the campers' field, flickered by pipistrelles
at nightfall, popping in and out of existence
like crackling eye-motes in Albert Einstein's
worst nightmares; tiny black holes
puncturing the Gore-Tex of the universe.
Physicists are ravenous for pathos.

Your passionate theories make me sick for apathy.
Turn the TV off. The screen goes black
as if the universe had had a heart attack,
cosmic cardiomyopathy;
infinite, starlit, hospital corridor;
reality's congenital disorder.

2

'Have I really been in a battle?' wondered Stendhal's hero after many hours blundering around the field of Waterloo, and many people today share a similar perplexity.
— Kenneth Minogue, *Alien Powers*

I

Alien powers: the vague forms of government
baffling the distance in-between
us like condensed breath. You are not alien
but your smile of greeting wafts into a grin
by that fumy air. You are all intent.

(Holding one's breath becomes the absolute,
the passive study of the other's face,
each mirror to a studied artifice,
in the pure, clear air; dirempt of force:
each mimicking the other's off-the-cuff salute.)

We meet underneath the spreading chestnut-tree
monographed by Eric Arthur Blair –
GO – so frequently the symbol for
a spontaneous order; and for nature
as meaningful, ultimate: smooth, planetary

fruits, webs, galactic with dew; the roots
a fretwork of dark-matter-arteries
reaching down through terrifying space
morphing infinitesimally into branches:
Jörgmungandr, the world-snake, swallowing its

own star-spangled tail. A fateful mistake.
I meet you in the Big House public bar
where you buy me... where you buy me a beer.
Cuchulaínn to my luckless Conchobar,
the alcohol enhances your mystique.

I see through ever-thickening goggles
the gold bling gangling all about your person,
possessed of a sudden, biblical passion
to flee the stony wilderness of Goshen
in a stretch limousine. The spirit boggles.

II

It's hard to see, now, admittedly... But
who, or what, does daylight represent?
Nothing but itself. Ah... how convenient:
something which is something and yet isn't —
the politics of God. You appear bright.

It's light, light, light with poets nowadays:
formless, colourless, weightless: a special plea
for state immunity. The thing's the play.
Hang your convex mirrors accordingly.
Cultivated in those daytime fantasies,

you are as honest as the day is long.
It's winter, though; hence the light is thin.
Consider the day-star. Piotr Kropotkin
broods on the morality of prison
finding it everywhere around him, wanting —

the world as universal gulag
(terribly political, these Russians)
forcing strange, unwarranted confessions
from the faithful; pathetic conditions
held up against the horrors of the stalag.

You're not so green as you're cabbage-looking.
I'm speaking to you, not to some god —
though even anarchists, the minute they're dead,
are taken up, like sun into a thundercloud.
There's a town in southern Russia called Kropotkin.

III

So then, did we fight at Waterloo?
Or was it all a simulation, a demon's
video game — poor pixellated humans
thinking themselves players on an immense
three-dimensional stage? I want to tell you

it was all just a bad dream... But I can't.
I was bored shitless by Stendhal's novels.
A mirror walking down the road...? That reveals
only the warm smiles of the stylish devils
you knew already, you absolute saint.

And did I meet you under the spreading chestnut tree?
Was it only my imagination?
Justice may be the ultimate illusion,
like God, I admit that; yet still you shine
judiciously and all you say is true.

Sarcasm is the lowest form of wit
to them that have none. Here, shake my hand;
be my neoliberal confidant and friend,
a powerless friendship, sound as a pound.
Maybe nobody will really get it.

Midwinter sun erupts like a phoenix'
egg in the trees' dense nest of branches.
But that's by the by. Escape those clutches.
Whatever germinates and hatches
hatches into the blind, chirruping hunger of fanatics.

3

I

Unquiet spirit, why do you vex
me with non-ex-
istence, King of France Complex,

whisper, doggedly, of not-quite-being,
and thereby bring
yourself about, as from a Big Bang

(or Tiny Pop) darkness
out of darkness
like a black hole? Maybe a weakness

or loophole in logic
made you, a necessary magic,
out-of-nothing cabaret-trick,

self-production from the self-same sleeve:
a dazzling move
even for The Great Jehovah,

stylish as a clinching paradox,
omnipotent sex
in various superpositions. Vex

me no longer, spirit.
Be quiet.
Ah, but then again... Speak, parrot.

Squawk and squawk again those cosmic echoes;
be a big noise,
spirit. Throw my own voice

denying your existence
like CERN's
ghost-whispers of undetectable protons.

II

Imagine I received this poem
from myself, a time-
traveller from the future, on a beam

of faster-than-light; and presuming that
I didn't write it
then – then, who the hell *did* write it?

Imagination's nowhere near enough,
not for all of
a century: a century of grief

morphing, jiltily, into an age of fear.
Explain the era
as a bad day in the Planetary Year;

dance, dance, with your great clodhoppers
on the paupers'
graves, the ploughed fields of Ypres,

Passchendaele and Somme;
plant a bomb
for the Arab Spring. I want my mum.

Not even Spielberg can
go all the way back to the Battle of the Marne.
Foul spirit, begone,

leave me to my dread
of your image: who appeared
as God's rainbow in the shattered eyes of the dead.

III

Were you there, spirit, in the school canteen?
Where 1940s schoolchildren
sucked the oxygen

back into the past:
coiffured and unevacuated, each gasmask
for a face, the punctured gasp,

the... general... ambience...
But our grandparents
are still alive... Behold, the disappearance

of the invisible:
of people who were never people.
How on earth, then, to unthink the unthinkable?

I don't know what you are, or what you mean,
spirit, other than
to lead me on (and on and on)

up the stairs
to that forbidden place,
the first to see its padlocked double doors,

to breathe its heavy, ancient air,
press to the shatterproof glass panes and stare
at what's not there.

(Grandad was an orphan,
with his Father, now, in heaven
when I don't think about it. Which is often.)

4

I

The dog, embarrassed, hunched on the pavement,
looks up at me with all the childlike despair
of the very old. A knot of dog-poo
untangles itself. It simply doesn't
not know where to look. Dumbly eloquent,

eyes glared upon, I stare back down at it
in my predominating human way,
white winter sun hanging in the lower
echelons of sky – almost a Lowry,
if Lowry had been the type to own a pet,

if he hadn't been a rent-collector,
if he'd done emotion; if he'd ever felt
the animal humanity of guilt.
I've never seen a blue-eyed dog before.
Bolted to the concrete, it yearns to bolt –

to bolt down, even, the body of the deed.
Its eyes deepen inward, looking downward,
suddenly three-dimensional in spirit –
like the best man who dirtied the room's good-
will, glug by glug, and suddenly knew it,

those ranges of silverwhite heads sighing
hurricanes to the poor bastard's hearing:
a forcefield of dumb sensitivity,
as the child at his first nativity
lowers his eyes while the angels gleam and sing.

II

Translucent fingerprints; the urine-
coloured liquid unsettling in the glass.
Hubbub-babble, bubbles. My lords, ladies
and gentlemen, a toast – to the bride's arse!
I must say, I found the speech a bit daring

for my taste. My blood. My water. My money.
Pouring out, full of all uncleanness
to a murmurous river – cacophony
rinsed out by nervous gulps of Guinness,
antiseptic sloshes of Bellini.

III

Society, I ween, may be judged
by the distance one keeps from one's own shit.
And others'? Naturally. Interpret
your slight distaste as sore travail of heart
when the champagne flute is handed to you smudged.

Please welcome to the room, Fergal and Eva!
The best man, wrecked with the Irish Rover,
sits on, alone, weeping blood and whiskey.
(The noonday demon is your hangover.)
Opinion poll – the speech was a bit... *risqué.*

It's all gone to buggery. Press a kiss
to the skin of the afflicted; it drives them mad.
But look, the pitiful are pitiless
in their refusals. Take Christ, for badness,
turning cheeky to Caesar and disgusting Herod

in the robe of scorn, like a child in adult
clothes laughing back at you, clean mirror of guilt;
Christ and Herod, horrible, both, taboo
as the mortifying touch of dog-poo.
I see it in her face, I see her feel it

through the thin plastic of the plastic bag-
cum-glove. Into the dustbin. Shtum.
Fixated by the ineffable dog
crushed by the weight of self-awareness all this time
inexpressibly, eloquently dumb,

the woman sees me with a look that talks
the language of animals – a language
faster than words, deeper than thought, in which
pity and commandment are bite and bark.
For the love of Jesus, will you fuckin walk?!

5

The lights! Turned on by a celebrity
in almost-human form, the hallelujah
of power (that which thrills you to a trance, e.g.
Rumpelstiltskin shaking hands with the mayor)
twitching with galvanic energy,
erecting an international city

of brief moment... In the moment it takes
for glitter to spaff out and die away.
Bosch! There goes your Northern Renaissance
in a blink, you might say, of the mind's eye;
this world and another seen in parallax
ever-so-briefly. Hung in that balance,

The Garden of Earthly Delights holds up
a strangely indecipherable mirror
to Coral Island and the Palace Discotheque.
Once I saw someone pissing against the bar
while ordering a pint, the garish dark
warding off the evil eye of Cyclops.

Fuck it, as they say: 'they' being POETS;
swearing pegged as authenticity
writ small, the clobber of the 'working-class'.
Here we go again. Alice's looking glass
presents the very image of the city
in fogged shards, refusing to coalesce,

lion and unicorn rampantly stand-offish.
Go state-of-the-nation on the nation-state
as it now stands: osteoarthritic,
Zimmer-framed. Everyone's a critic:
jabber's Jabberwocky, vorpal, uffish.
What makes you think you're so flipping great?

It is a disrelation to power
that vomits back a bitter piety.
The lights go out again on Central Pier,
the big wheel stops turning. It's you I see
in the darkness, staring up at the Tower,
lost to yourself in strange Utopia.

6

It is time, then, for you to take a little mild and pleasant nourishment which by being absorbed into your body will prepare the way for something stronger. Let us bring to bear the persuasive powers of sweet-tongued rhetoric, powers which soon go astray from the true path unless they follow my instructions. And let us have as well Music, the maid-servant of my house, to sing us melodies of varying mood.
— Boethius, *The Consolation of Philosophy* (trans. Victor Watts)

I

Of varying mood, the tree-tops whisper-hiss their choric
        spontaneities
through my open window – a *sweet-tongued rhetoric*
        of tuneless ditties

as the wind strikes up. Melody as rhythm, and vice versa,
        the branches' subtle
disputations: philosophy's shekere, cabasa,
        the wind's rattle

of mute persuasive powers. I wonder if Boethius
        in his prison
heard through his own high window such a breathy, breathless
        diapason

as this, a desperate wind leafing through the canopies,
        and filled up.
They have no medicines to ease his pains… Quite a mouthful, this,
        of the bitter cup.

II

No squirrels today. The branches' skittering genius,
        so to speak,
in hiding, conjuring the image of a universe
        at hide and seek

with itself. A baby's peekaboo: the innocent fun
        of Brahma
in its googolplex of costumes, lost in its very own
        improvised drama.

Whatever that implies, it isn't something all of
        us can agree on,
the self as *ultima realitas*. But you forget yourself.
        Each hour an eon

of the clock, the self-winding journey; your trillionth
        step leads somewhere else
for the trillionth time, plodding the bureaucratic labyrinth
        of Kali's bowels.

III

Follow the money! as they seem to say. But what is it —
        and where can it go
from here? Nonsense verse of neoliberal diktat
        against sorrow,

the drip-drip-dripping canopy of the prison ceiling.
        Boethius'
walls were not walls, he was no prisoner. I am struggling
        to believe this.

IV

Here, on the lowest plane, sometimes you'll spot a rat's
        tentative surge
across open ground, disappearing then among the roots'
        holdings, the garbage

slumping from the bins. Summer's hot this year. The yard exudes
        a poisonous smell,
the kind that stains the throat brown for minutes afterwards
        like leaking petrol,

bites in the middle of your head like a repressed memory
        loth to come out.
For mortal beings, the underworld is temporary.
        The faint taste of rot

in warm air, fertile odours; trees muscular, overgrown;
        a nameless martyr
hanging with gross distorted face, in propria persona
        non grata.

V

I am no prisoner. Call that statement perlocutionary.
        Among such wealth
how is one not free? Your Google search *how to painlessly
        kill yourselth*

hyper-, not auto-, corrected. I float in blessing's bubble.
        The air is stuffy,
unconditioned. The window is loose-jawed, the tree-tops garble
        their philosophy.

VI

If you can't say something nice, don't say anything at all.
        Sorry, mum.
Let's start again here, try to say something original
        to end the poem

for good: something about creation and destruction
        dancing together
in endless blackout. When I ask, you speak to distraction
        of your poor mother

trudging the miles to Balzan, cradling the delicacies
        of new-born eggs
in her dress; a natural cussedness abiding curses.
        Old ideologues,

Mussolini's rhetoric, Churchill's, fading into Mintoff's,
        your body's *terra*
irredenta — what can that avail your alien griefs,
        outlandish horror?

I still see from a child's perspective. Maybe we all do
        and we always will.
Even at seventy, you're walking hand in hand to Birgu
        as a little girl

to a saint's feast, the fireworks on, in, the black water,
        skittish, mesmeric:
destruction and creation, dancing drunkenly together
        at a child's music.

7

I

No more of that:
deliberated movements unbecoming of themselves,
becoming someone else's, someone else,
deliberate-

-ly tightrope-
stumbling the dashed lines in the middle of the road;
dancing a shambly, hypertrophied
two-step

who walks it
all the way from town on a Friday night, ready to drop,
star-like, out of constellation Europe
(knowledge of Brexit

nobbling opinion).
Cat's eyes cataracting, a huge downpour blanks you
watering the ground with mordant urine,
channelling Banksy

's anonymous
ubiquity; a ubiquitous anonymity
rising like damp in each subsiding city
house by house.

Losing track
here could prove fatal. Your lucky break is broken
across the line, across which you're taken
by a lucky break

into a blind field —
floundering in that primal matter, or chaos
of mud, where universal darkness
shines, revealed.

II

No more of what?
That first section didn't make it particularly clear.
Nevertheless — the wind shakes out
the rain's mantilla

black with leaves,
traffic advances its cortege to walking pace;
in the bus shelter a people grieves
its expected bus.

The world is small
enough to imagine: endlessly recycled weather
ghost-written by a nameless author
of muted appeal,

pathetic fallacies
of logic: I am not the world's to mirror, it is mine.
December sky gives up its slow design,
crumples to pieces

what was gathered
in the dark. An autobiography
captured in ice-puddles, my reflection briefly
illustrates the dead —

the living, that is,
a shadow on the lens. The history of elegy
obverts the elegy of history,
Eros and Thanatos'

unhappy marriage.
Anyone'd think they keep us waiting here on purpose.
Immaculate sunshowers turn the page
to foul papers.

III

No more of this
petitioning for existence. Maybe it's a good sign
when you're generally ignored, condign
to a powerlessness

bearing out the day:
not deleted, quite, but marginally justified.
As pulpy nestlings gulp their Twitter-feed
tweet your birth-cry.

I hear a peacock's
cry, see shimmering forms of transmigrated men and women
calling desperately to foreign children.
Something on Netflix

perhaps or YouTube
transported me, flung through the wormhole of a diode.
By the time you read this, I will have died.
Do Not Disturb

my profile. Shakespeare
wanted ubiquity and anonymity at once,
achieved it: a oneness of presence,
that clear-as-air

transfiguring mask.
If you can't see it, maybe shut up and listen.
Consider the self-abasing passion
of Sacher-Masoch

for utopia.
I've a sentimental passion for the work of bell hooks,
the fury of the black-boned phoenix
drinking the fire.

IV

No more of these
unnerving displays. Everyone got over their afflictions,
enshrined, happily, in their higher factions –
I mean faculties

(Freudian slip) –
eminent, online, adverting one and all to their
smooth recoveries. A rising culture:
the sweet dollop

of unsavoury
leaven, supplementary quintessence of a rough
artisan's bread. (Inflation of your dough
will vary.)

Let them eat
bread, choose from our exciting new range of sailor's rations.

Change tack. Grow stately as a Russian's
monarchy of wheat.

(Sun overhang-
ing winter trees, skimped with ivy, lights briefly as if
reanimated – come back to life
with a silent bang)

Inconvenience
of the world's breath. The world is everything that is
the case (since that's the case). Among these
kindling thespians

find yourself cast
as dead wood; discover yourself therein, a red-
hot clinker puffing up the bread
of Culture Fest.

V

(No more, no more...)
That'll do, *thank* you! Don't call us, we'll... Just don't call us.
Eyes down for your last flourish, soulless
exit through stagedoor.

EXTERIOR: DAY:
SRI KRISHNA RAVAGING THE ADMINISTRATIVE CLASSES
WITH HURRICANES OF FIRE. Such vacancies
direct your play.

From a bar-room
music splashes like a slop, the door bangs to again
with a kick of storm, spat spats of rain,
wind's boom-boom

with a rouzled earth;
space unfolding from its narrow box, heaven's disorder.
When heaven kills a thing it isn't murder,
or even death:

heterogeneous
infinities resolve into an image of the actual
and part again. That's questionable.
It takes a genius

beyond intelligence
to play well with others: even one's own creations
might rise up and bite with admonitions
of common sense.

Leave it to the gurus.
On the outskirts of the city, a festival of god
or celebration of the burning flood.
Drown like sorrows.

8

It means, 'Look, this is the world that looks so dangerous. It is child's play, it is only right to make a joke about it!'
— Sigmund Freud, 'Humour'

Sappho, who wrongs you?
— Sappho, 'Ode to Aphrodite'

Humour is reality's base element –
or consciousness is, as some claim, the two things
entangled; or – stronger than that – they're the same –
if only we knew! –

self-experience a wild get-together
buzzing with silly strings, unlistenable
music; quagmires of bottomless quantum foam
curdling the dancefloor,

jelly and ice-cream mounting the horizon...
Frozen in time, perhaps; or, better still, set
like a grin. A clown's grin, mind you – melting from
laughter to terror!

—

Requests for something halfway 'palatable'
to help myself get on, or at least for you,
my traumatised fiancée, who rebuffs me
like a worn-down coin,

I don't find it easy: 'non disputandum' –
after ten cramped years of being spoon-force-fed
crap society? I paint with a palette
of intricate browns,

wall-curlicues of what lurks deepest in me.
Invoke the IRA at personal cost.
Highlight all and press delete – or else highlight
pressure's deletions.

—

Great weather for plants: sunshine impeached by rain
prorogued by sunshine; the zoetrope of sky
dark to light to dark, your stultified movements'
comedy routine.

The Day of the Triffids? Of the rabblement –
slobbing their tendrils; slug-trailing, uprooted;
translated from your soiled, rust-brambled borders
right to your doorstep.

At large in the North, the red squirrel's famous
tragic destiny – perennial species?
hardy aliens? – implants the metaphors
of nature in frack.

—

(The poem hypnotises like a vampire –
sucks me dry, loth to unstick. I am sorry.
The heart shakes me as if through blood-profusion
or evil passion.)

Paggered by the recent rainstorm, a May-tree
has shed its infantile pink blood of petals.
A flat pool lies under it, a flat pink pool
of delicate blood.

Tie it together, if your dexterity
of wrung faith allows you. I hereby hand you
this ceremonial glut of May-petals
instead of my life.

—

Butylone in the blood, ketamine, cocaine
in the brain, I poured myself out to unhinged
toilets; the house's lights neither on nor off,
nobody not home –

the *Marie Celeste* relayed by a cousin
with rough English. *And, there, nobody there was!*
Unhasp the bald patch to inspect the damage;
the neural porridge

stirred to inaction. Whip me up a grey froth.
Society's complex blood evolved to boil
on introduction, its every somebody
an antibody.

—

Poetry is imaginative revenge.
It didn't start that way. When I was a kid
I wrote a poem in four-stress rhymed couplets
on a butterfly

that was pinned to the classroom wall; fluttering
anapaests, pretty winged thing, ITS IMAGERY
AND RHYTHMS WENT VERY WELL WITH THE SUBJECT!
Is that what you want?

—

(Light to dark to light: hypnagogic eyelids;
vision taking off, landing; sensory limbs
of trees your mind touches on, stimming and still:
shelter's tortoiseshell.)

—

Reality is humour's base element.
Look at this: everything but the kitchen sink
throwing the drama; what I don't know being
what I'm on about,

blind hostage on my 'emotional journey'
from A to B – Amusement to Bemusement –
and not the other way around: comedy
in the cosmic sense

(not the divine sense). But enough about me.
Reality is humour's base element...
Let's try that again, in a sense that the old
repeats are timeless.

—

Caveat emptor. Don't buy the fenced-around
rhetoric of nation: ever your English
dead in the breach, groundlings in for a penny
squozen in the pound.

Powerful stuff, that stuff, the stuff of power,
played to the gallery, or played to the gods –
benevolent autocracy in its robes
of wrapping paper.

—

Metaphors have become my windows, windows
my metaphors. Body in many a room
I stare out of habit out of habitus
into the same world

as my own, as anyone's except my own.
Fantastic administrative vacancies!
Rain tremulous as a spider's-web-curtain
lifting from a tomb.

—

I try to follow thoughts away into sleep
but they hear me following, hear me hearing,
thunk back into me. The stunned mind telescopes
back into itself.

The mind its own predator, a stereo-
typical music biting on loop-the-loop –
the unconscious won't slink out to outfox me
with unconsciousness.

Words and images pinging off each other,
neurons in the void; dying till 5am;
the blinds' blades glistening with the grim beauty
of a requiem.

—

Consciousness I imagine as a mushroom:
ceramic-fleshed, the phoenix's golem,
blaring out of decay; itself a symbol
of – yes, you guessed it –

consciousness; mushroom; phoenix; consciousness;
an infinitely germinating sequence
going nowhere, leaving much to be desired
and much to be said.

What is to be desired is not to be said.
Desire to think is not thinking to desire.
Consciousness I imagine as a mushroom
hallucinating.

———

Elementals humour base reality.
Spacetime as story-time to eternity,
lulling to sleep immortal baby daughters
doing the voices;

loving indulgence as we would have wished it,
had we known it; had we known them, known ourselves,
new-faced parents gurgling up at themselves
imago Dei –

the gods of love whose faces are as mirrors.
Once upon a time there was a fairy-tale
in which the mirror spoke. Maybe you heard it;
maybe you didn't.

———

They would almost certainly ape the characteristics of the state
power brokers they lobby vociferously, and be able to fit in
comfortably at a top level networking event.
— Oli Mould, *Against Creativity*

Trade in your semi-colons for ellipses
at the bank of social credit; dine out on
your current account; let them appreciate
your self-investment.

State power brokers state their power broken.
Waving at you – at the networking event,
in the vociferous lobby – is the sight
of one hand clapping.

—

Monomaniacal: – the storm's brevity
of inexplicable enthusiasm
for an earth which never even remotely
interested it –

dark outbursts of rain, insisting resistance,
on everything an unforgiving presence –
from which a bird hops under a car to hide
like an old sinner.

—

I can see the sunset but without the sun
sounds like something from an Instagram poem
but isn't. Really. I can see the sunset
but without the sun.

—

Michael the angel with his filleting knife
patrolling the green depths of the playing fields
chain-knotted with swings swinging half-perspectived
in and out of sight

ticking off the Park's defensive formations
of batter-faced houses corralled and at bay
windows occasionally flicks a shadow
like a fish's blink

through a great invisible cell of water
so far with nothing between them like the one
he saw that time on a school trip to Sea Life
called the angelfish.

—

Cemetery autumn. Things are looking up –
stop looking down, then, at leaves clumping your feet.
Or so the dead say, absently, lit by clear-
eyed October sun

concentrating them like a thorny crossword.
Crosses and words. FALLEN ASLEEP IN THE FLESH,
or RESTING NOW WITH JESUS. Resurrection
as the *certain hope*;

the life-befuddling clue, the flummoxed martyr...
I can feel them bubbling the top of my head,
the ever-rising faces; the idea;
the aspiring dead.

—

To the person about to jump at Leeds train station,
30th of May 2019 (2pm–3pm)

As I write this you may have jumped already
the heart's breakneck from the bridge to the train-track
enough to kill, to leave your guilty body
a 'gross intrusion'

on private property. This is how it's billed
– TRAINS CANCELLED DUE TO TRESPASSERS ON THE LINE –
though you haven't jumped yet, your trespass proclaimed
unforgiveable,

causing disruption to your onward journey.
MAN SPOTTED IN 'PRECARIOUS POSITION'...
Man passes, with last word, from euphemism
into blasphemy.

9

The disordered family is full of dutiful children.
The disordered society is full of loyal patriots.
— *Tao Te Ching* (trans. Ursula Le Guin)

I

Not that I care, stirring the new tea
so hard I break the tea-
bag, though why it was left in
remains murky, so its bitty spores,
its cacky spoors,
mount the cup with darkening tannin
like a sudden manifestation of the Tao;

not that I notice the miniature
whirlpool, no, vortex, of char,
or each tiny plant-fibre
risen to the excitement of my spoon
in dizzy spin
of gravity, it seems, slight forebear
of a physics I neither notice nor endure,

neither acknowledge nor deny,
maybe as a chai-
wallah lacking the feel of it,
a public notary without the ritual.
Not that I fail
in my not failing, or in the effort
not to try, but the natural impulse to try

harder next time now suffuses me,
infuses, confuses me.
How should I do better at stirring
the tea? A cleaner, a purer medium,
that whole storm; some
way of doing it, a way of not doing
contained, somehow, in this ruined cup of Tetley's tea.

II

Instantly the medium reverts —
retorts, back to its
unstirring state, a vortexless
entropy of little brown floaters.
A stillness that flatters
my sense of things; whirled on its axis
round that microcosmic world-pool fraught with dark bits,

returned. The ego of the tea-mug.
Little death of teabag.
Dispersing in the tea's hot grief
like a mascara-crumbed, half-private blubbing;
a surface bobbing
with evident regret, the lost tealeaf —
reasserting equilibrium, dreg by dreg.

III

Not that you care, even, I would guess,
taking tea in a glass,
your Earl-Grey-lapsang-souchong
sea of silvermilk tranquillity,
chai latte

serenity, seen sugar-sashaying
in it, settling there like a sweet spirit in bliss;

or that you'd notice, drinking green tea
in a goblet, or mate
greenery of Latin America
jungling the concrete cavern of your mouth...
Delicious myth,
with fairytale ending of iced mocha;
all beautifully ordered as your society.

IV

Interpretations of 'The Prologue
of the Broken Teabag'
abound. An industry is risen.
(Already.) Ten thousand exegetes drink
black ink
sweetened with bile; each in the prison
of her intellect, in solitary dialogue.

Past present and future interlag
in the broken teabag
in ways no one can finally explain.
Controversies of the warring schools
tip the scales
west to east, and east to west again —
unbalanced by that currency currently in vogue.

At the bottom of the cup the clag
of the broken teabag
suggests an age of divination.
Ten thousand scholars peer in at the rim
and prophets come.

Its fibres grit the white teeth of nations
and in the morning wind fly brown and tattered flags.

V

Four white horses with royal-blue crowns
clatter and bounce
by, pulling a white carriage-hearse.
From where I stand its progress looks
almost inex-
plicably clear; traffic lights, pedestrians, cars
as quibbles put to the judgement of a great presence.

How do you follow that? No one is.
Behind the hearse-
carriage, traffic smoothly remembers
itself, or is smoothly remembered;
the main road
is main again, white horses, white hearse,
vanished into all observers' pasts and futures.

The afternoon is the decade's last.
It seems rehearsed,
as if none of it were possible
unless imagined; the coffin empty;
peremptory
flash of a moment, a child's fable
in which the ever-after is discovered to be lost.

You wonder don't you, or do you,
where it's off to
in its jaunting gravity of haste;
and not just how it leaves, but what it leaves,
like broken tealeaves'
bitter residue, a darkening taste,
or a sudden manifestation of the Tao.

10

Marzu marzellu, iftakh il bieb u ir-rixtellu!

I

March the tenth, tenth day of spring's first month,
the air a humming, apocalyptic clarity,
TO THE THIRTEENTH-
CENTURY CHURCH OF THE HOLY TRINITY
through the Roman-Viking-Northern labyrinth

of York: half-lost there, time out of mind,
and the Minster in its supernatural mass
afloat in the ground,
a kingdom of kaleidoscopic darkness
open on the real world; paradise retained;

godlike interior, excessive mysteries...
Where I go to lose myself, the Minister!
Memory belies
the Great East Window, a monster
eating the light. While you're in there, that is —

rejects you, zooplankton that you are,
your life is passed over in a dazzled gloom.
Now then, where
are we? *A-whole-nother millennium*
away from where I started, wherever

that was, not even that long ago:
the air's apocalyptic clarity
a glacial overflow

bearing us out, shocked in its purity —
bodies new-revealed, wherever they will go.

II

God preserve you, Margaret Clitherow;
crocus, daffodil, chrysanthemum,
preserve also.
Vividly dead, we may yearn to press them
for an answer, in the slim folio

of your life, the heavy bindings of Apocalypse.
We're out of time. Would you like to ask
me a question, perhaps?
as you might say. I see the surgical facemask
the a la mode of imminent collapse.

Shall we talk about the pandemic to come —
ten million deaths from Covid-19,
the sour-smelling doom
shambling towards us, turned out of your shrine
with a tart phrase: *Miss Margaret's not home?*

Zombie-pilgrims at the end of their road
bumble-bump at the door of your conscience,
misericord
and altar: your secret place, whose every silence
preserves, implausibly, a thin air of God.

III

March thirteenth, thirteenth day of much-
benighted spring, lightfingered stealing in

to the dark church:
the relics of corruptible England
tricked out by the shape, shadowy and rich.

Revelation's old myths: the unveiling
of forms, dimensions, each upward curve, eyes
on the cryptic ceiling;
space filling out like a director's tease.
There is nothing permanent here to belong

to. The book of life, thoroughly opaque
as church-windows, coming anxiously to light,
full of dark
matter, energy... I dearly depart.
Clouds command again the wapentake.

IV

Skip through the audiobook of life
to the end, the dry rasping of the last leaves
(subtitled for the deaf
and hard of hearing). What is it grieves
but the god's-eye drama of our own grief,

angled at ourselves by Lakshmi's mirror?
By us, I mean postfuturist, posthistoric
Europe: there we are
in the bone-pit, selfie-posing with the skull of Yorick,
grave hyperbole the live furor.

V

York to Jorvik, Yorick, back to York.
City of encircled time, ticking along.
Tick tick tick
go the daffodils. The buds gyrate. Spring,
the prehistory of the future, the buzzing clock.

11

I hope this finds you safe and well at this uncertain time.

You find me (if you do) in the spare room, at the desk, road, cars, trees transpearing in the window;

the window my fourth wall, the fourth wall of a prison drama; an imaginary wall: the imagination walled up with windows, the prisoner's panopticon.

Half the world a captive audience, topping the plague bill, under cordial arrest, encased in glass and brick and broadband: a clearer, more indeterminate setting you couldn't wish for in the sovereign and splendidly appointed house of prose.

...

Society, the open cell, of cloddering, yeasty air:

our over-extended nation, shut up; the family dog, closed in by human clangour in the glasshouse.

Top dog as cat: its window of opportunity, fronting directly our locked, inopportune windows, wide open, commanding its prospects, its bailey of bushes, trees, barbed snarling coil;

the air so reasty and so rammish with intelligence of cat it makes your head swell, your eyes pop, your skin crackle, your nose melt, your brain dry up into moon-concrete, your blood thicken and your lungs collapse (among other symptoms)...

...

A cross but lately gracing my pown, bepowlert shoulders.

Poetry may be the fairer house for isolation, with more and greater windows, as Emily Dickinson said;

garden-landscapes glimpsed in epic morphologies of sun and shadow, puppeting the glass, red squirrels frisking down their hierarchies (boughs, branches, twigs)

wood-pigeons peerless, pontificalibus in gutters; God's creation a child's encyclopaedia. Metaphor, the power of the glimpse, the glimpsed power, proportionate to the attic-world's plush poverty of proportion. I recommend her letters, if you haven't read them already.

...

And Thomas Nashe, his writing always plagued in some way,

plaguing, plaguey; within, against, about, and for the Black Death, circulating London's draffish blood;

penny-pamphlets tearing through throwaway
populations; language mutating, infecting, against the
plague of silences, bedizening its dark foreground like the
royal progress of a snail.

What he worked in animated, plagued; death became him.
Resistance is febrile. And, yes, that is applicable to life, O
Universities, these are transferable skills; human resources
drained, hobbledehoyed by rusting supply chains and our
sores infected.

...

Style being style of being, a continual failure, it
discontinues

suddenly: and in that opening – maybe a window, if
pushed – reality blanks and you copy yourself down.

Not to overdo it: you have to reach that nadir before the
landscape, its quiet road, its overgrown undergrowth,
that mimsy sebaceous cat, revolve into view.

It's always existential: which is to say, to force something
into being it has to nix your own, in some small way (you
hope). And what more sufficient medium for the triumph
of failure than whatever voice you're hearing in your
head right now?

...

Not to make of myself a Kabbalistic pseudo-Jehovah

sucking in his infinite gut, making a modicum of spacetime
for the real to squeeze through, awkwardly,

avoiding eye contact at all cost, holding its breath; or
lifting the sash to free the frampold wasp. You might
object, I might object, to a false picture there; and you, I,
might be right.

Maybe it's more like grasping something so hard it grafts
agonisingly into the palm of your hand and enjoins your
fingers and becomes both you and something else like the
fruit that, adamantined in your grip, mushes you to pulp
and pith, turns your heart-stone to flesh –

...

But anyway.

What I want to know is, how are you? How've you been
coping with the isolation? How's things?

Are you enjoying the quiet time, the slow gigantic
movements in the dome? Well you might say, if questions
were horses, beggars would ride – well, yes –

begging the question hoarse was always my rider. Am
I, or is humanity, the spider? I could spin the web out
indefinitely, for sure, but we may not have time; though
infinite space may be inferred in a nutshell, it may grow
up, in time, a hazel tree.

...

Springtime, lest we forget! Who'd 'a thunk it?

Pan, our old tutelary genius, in his latest overegged comeback, letting slip his surname?

Like that time your teacher at school leaked her first name to the class, and suddenly, secretly, unexpectedly, you choked? When you were psychically immune and a bit too old?

Butterflies blot the air, creamy drip-drops on reality's hinter-cloth; bees return to their promised land to make the milk and honey. I don't know about you. I think of huge Indian texts, rainbow-woven mythographies, rolled up, rotting sedately on the shelves of empty manor houses

...

unrolling now on romthsome oak tables, heaved out

by ghosts of the kaliyuga; purifying the listener, the enquirer, and the speaker, purifying the three worlds.

Earth, riddled with evil, goes off to the Creator for a cure, big cow eyes sharpened with tears: Krishna, born to Devakī, the virgin, the outcome. (Take prescription as read.)

Born into house arrest, locked down by Kamsa, the ill-favouring, ill-favoured king. The eighth son will kill him,

allegedly: so he murders each of her new-borns, one by
one, for some reason (erring greatly on the side of power,
as power does)

...

Krishna, the inevitable eighth-born, spirited away –

the god-boy smuggled out to the royal family up-country,
unknown to them, swapped in for their daughter:

Yogamaya, born the same day, who's then slaughtered
in his place, Kamsa scutching her like a whip against the
stone, baby head exploding like a firework –

spirit shooting to heaven, bleeding out into sunset,
goddess of illusion. And the boy would surprise them, at
times, not knowing his nature, like when he yawned and
Yaśodā, his foster-mum, glimpsed in his tiny toothless
mouth all matter and all living things.

...

Under the cool shade of women, by the Jumna River
(Uttar Pradesh);

innocently total, effortless against monsters, the baby's
wide-eyed omnipotence at focus in the world;

horseplay, acting the goat, pulling the tails of monkeys, he
and Balarama, the elder of the two, fizzgigging through

the deep green forest, the delight of Gokula;

gathered round the dark-skinned boy, a pericarp of friends, of thousands, bright in the clearing, the lotus's heart, radiating petals, pollenating the bees, his song fermenting in the steamy air, sunlight and honey, intoxicating, extempore, in perfect time, in a world of his own.

...

Through many legends of flabbergasting childish power

to adulthood, 'the age of justice', his father kidnapped by another evil-wisher suddenly popped up

making Krishna cry out on fate, that new normal, a tantric tantrum of powerlessness; the Creator 'creating', as they used to say up north. *Stop creatin'*.

Stop carrying on. The story ends with the world's panacea, Krishna, who is himself the world, withdrawing himself from himself for his own good: a theology of government advice, the crabbed prescription. Lord, have mercy on us. My god, is that the time.

April – May 2020

12

I

Sunday morning and the builders are here
taking over my living-room window.
Just heads, at first, popping up, then higher
as the scaffolding takes shape and the whole view
is commandeered at last, each boxered arse
pointing back down at me like Caravaggio's horse.

A classic at the altar of the people!
I don't know who these people are: with each glance
in our eyes shiftily grapple
for right of aversion, that dominance
of dictatorial embarrassments,
each voice throwing the other in its silence

though far from silent, these early fuckers,
hammering in profanities with nailgunnish
repetitive speed, scattergunning focus.
Just to ask — when will all this be finished?
Here today, mate, then in some future
life we'll come back to do the guttering and fascia.

Funny... How the prospect of things ending
makes them near impossible to begin,
how things end with visions of beginning;
imaginable, now, with the mooning workmen,
their scaffolding rampant in the window
rattled by it, swearing blow by blow,

skeletal leaves wreathing round their heads
like the year's lost money. Early autumn.
The garden, gold-silvery, divests its assets;
summer's lightness sinking to the bottom
of the world, the sky's grey reservoir
sucking down the light and closing over.

The dead stirring in those vertical depths.
I know each droplet in that cloud is condensed
on a speck of dust, a million tiny deaths
to set my fast-benumbing face against:
vapours risen from the earth and coalesced
in clouds around those galaxies of dust.

II

After a week a squirrel curvet-cavorts
like a medieval comic actor
on the scaffold; till a magpie alights,
chasing it from the stage, the plague doctor
glossy-black-gowned, trim-booted, plastic-beaked.
An allegory I myself enact

with the builders gone, their backdrop on the change,
as well, with the season's impetus,
what leaves remain now a frazzled orange
clinging on; can't not evoke the impotence
of progress, blasting out the Last Trump
in widescreen view of colour-draining swamp –

exit stage left, shedding withered leaves –
less King Lear and more King Ubu,
a tragi-com satirising the lives
of its audience. *Taboo, or not taboo…*

Meanwhile the rain proceeds to nibble
with growing comfort at the water table.

Mushrooms peep up out of the lazy grume.
Squirrels, panicked investors, bury
their little windfalls, forgetting the last time
the weather turned. And every time. History
runs on, the time is never upon us,
treading water in the air like Adonis

pursued (hotly) across the cold-steamy fields
of desire; an ecstatic Venus
hard on our heels, never upon us.
Never that final clinching of the worlds.
Comedy's (red-hot) delay of action
makes dilection endless predilection,

gives to the momentous its momentum,
momentum moment and momentousness,
the masterful teasing out of orgasm,
foreplay as sex's apotheosis –
history a scaffold of desire
you can't step off, though the gods love a trier.

III

Venus hearts Adonis. She has stuck
by him through stanza after stanza
of body-language and he doesn't give a fuck.
If she's a question, he is not the answer.
There's a funny kind of call and response
between her voice and his echoing silence.

Adonis hearts Adonis; apparently:
his self-security the bloodless mask
of the flesh-reddening terror making him flee
the answer that the question lives to ask.
The mind scuttles underneath the settee
dogging itself in wet avidity.

Venus hearts Venus; but hearts Adonis
despite herself, despite him, because of herself
and him; despite the lolling penis
of his body; a blood-lusty she-wolf
fantasising the passive blob of a sheep.
But when she collapses in anaemic sleep

in front of him, he bends to her to beg
the question of her unresponsive love.
I've always loved you... They dissolve. Dog
and wolf, tame and wild, run through them both, alive,
each in the other satisfied and famished:
a lovers' history, happily finished.

IV

My language squirms in teenage gaucherie
at being seen and needing to be seen.
Auditioned and auditioning: chary
of show, of showing its need to be shown,
making a real show of its chariness —
the poem cringes at the reader's kiss.

I want you and don't want you at the same time.
No idea what the ending is yet,
but we're almost there. I'm almost there. I'm
struggling to keep the mind free of it.

The little yellow snake of my resentments
puts out my tongue in venomous silence.

(I wandered lonely as a cloud of toxin
sprouting like a death-cap from the I.C.I.
strangling the roots and filling the dykes in
with rotten sludge; watercolouring my
'hinterland' – the leap made, long fallen short –
in a caustic wash of dark, evil shit.)

Some time, now, since that early wake-up call.
The scaffolding, medievally sturdy,
is still here, the workmen gone: a skeletal
monument to the disappearing body.
Caught in a scaffold-web, a black feather
dances its macabre tarantella.

Maybe all I really want is to impress
you with the cool stamp of my authority;
to set my seal on you with every kiss
in panic as in careful poetry
(although to write these last lines is to wax
Fakespearean; see line five-one-six

of *Venus and Adonis*). Maybe I desire
something else, something too obvious to know,
clear as water in a bowl of black sapphire,
October night's dark, translucent window;
maybe what I want, with some want of skill,
is to say *I love you and I always will*.

A few notes to the poems

1

"*Teste David cum Sibylla*": words from the *Dies Irae* ('Day of Wrath'), a thirteenth-century poem-song in Latin which portends the end of the world and Last Judgement, in Roman Catholic-Christian terms. The line means something like "David witnessing with the Sybil". Portions of the text, including this line, are sung in Wolfgang Amadeus Mozart's *Requiem in D Minor*.
Euclid: 323-283BCE: founder of the discipline of geometry.

2

"King of France Complex": a reference to Bertrand Russell's famous statement "The present King of France is bald", there being, at the time of (Russell's) writing, no King of France.
Jörgmungandr: in Norse mythology, the snake which encoils the world, biting its own tail.
Cuchalaínn: hero of the Ulster cycle, including *The Cattle Raid of Cooley* – see *The Taín*.
Conchubar: King of Ulster in the Ulster cycle.
Piotr Kropotkin: Russian anarchist writer (1842-1921), author of *The Conquest of Bread* and *Mutual Aid*.

6

Brahma: the godhead of Hinduism. Pronounced 'brahma', in which the 'h' is a voiced glottal fricative [ɦ], with both syllables stressed. In other words, it is not a full rhyme with 'drama'.
Kali: in Hinduism, goddess of time and death, and presiding spirit of the current era.

Mintoff: Dom Mintoff, Prime Minster of Malta, 1955-58 and 1967-84.

7

bell hooks: author of *Bone Black: Memories of Girlhood, Feminism Is for Everyone, All About Love: New Visions*, etc.

Sacher-Masoch: Leopold von Sacher-Masoch, socialist utopian and author of *Venus in Furs*.

"SRI KRISHNA RAVAGING THE ADMINISTRATIVE CLASSES WITH HURRICANES OF FIRE."

Adapted from *Śrīmad-Bhagāvatam*.

9

Tao: the nameless fundamental principle of nature, affinity and harmony with which leads to *Te*, the (also untranslatable) state of effortless, natural, peaceful mastery of being.

"The way that can be spoken of
Is not the constant way.
The name that can be named
Is not the constant name."

"Do that which consists of taking no action, and order will prevail."

"I take no action and the people are transformed of themselves" – etc.

Tao Te Ching (trans. D.C. Lau)

This poem was written shortly after the United Kingdom's general election of December 2019.

10:

Epigraph: a Maltese proverb, roughly translating as 'March, hammer down the door and the gate!'

Margaret Clitherow: saint of the Roman Catholic church, martyred in York, England, 1586; pressed to death for refusing to plead – in order to protect her family, at least in part – regarding an accusation of harbouring Catholic priests. There is a shrine to her in her original house in The Shambles, York.

11

Thomas Nashe: writer of the late 1580s and 1590s; author of *Lenten Stuffe*, *Pierce Penniless His Supplication to the Devil*, *The Unfortunate Traveller*, etc.

"the delight of Gokula": taken from *Krishna: The Beautiful Legend of God* (Penguin, 2003, p. 41), which is Book 10 of *Śrīmad-Bhagāvatam*.

The narrative section dealing with Krishna's birth, youth, and maturity is an epitome of *Śrīmad-Bhagāvatam*. I have of course taken massive liberties in my condensing of this narrative, but I intend this section to be a tribute also to the wonders of the text as a whole (in particular the translation by Edwin F. Bryant, published as *The Beautiful Legend of God*).

Some of these poems have appeared previously in *Belle Ombre*, *Blackbox Manifold*, *PN Review*, and *Stand*.